*This book is dedicated to Casey Elle*
*and her children and their children and their children ...*
*Special thanks to our mums, Beryl and Gloria, and our friend Lesley Henry*

First published 1998 in the United States of America by
Charlesbridge Publishing
85 Main Street, Watertown, MA 02172-4411
(617) 926-0329

First published 1997 in Australia by
University of Queensland Press
Box 42, St Lucia, Queensland 4067

Printed in Hong Kong
(hc) 10 9 8 7 6 5 4 3 2 1
(sc) 10 9 8 7 6 5 4 3 2 1

**Library of Congress Cataloging-in-Publication Data**
Toft, Kim Michelle.
One less fish / Kim Michelle Toft and Allan Sheather; illustrations by Kim Michelle Toft.
p.     cm.
Summary: Counting down from twelve to zero, the reader learns about some of the fish found on
the Great Barrier Reef and the threats to their continued existence.
ISBN 0-88106-322-3 (reinforced for library use)
ISBN 0-88106-323-1 (softcover)
1. Counting—Juvenile literature. 2. Subtraction—Juvenile literature. 3. Fishes—Australia—
Great Barrier Reef (Qld.)—Juvenile literature. [1. Fishes. 2. Coral reef animals.
3. Environmental protection. 4. Great Barrier Reef (Qld.) 5. Counting.] I. Sheather, Allan.
II. Title.
QA113.T64      1997
513.2'12—dc21      97-23615

The illustrations in this book are done in ink and dyes on silk.
The display type and text type were set in ITC Benguiat Gothic by
Ads-Up Graphics Pty Ltd., Brisbane, Queensland, Australia.
Color separations were made by Hi Tech Graphics, Melbourne, Victoria, Australia.
Layout by Ads-Up Graphics Pty Ltd.
Printed and bound by South China Printing Co. (1988) Ltd.

# one less fish

Kim Michelle Toft and Allan Sheather
Illustrated by Kim Michelle Toft

 Charlesbridge

# 12 twelve

Twelve gracious angelfish
thinking they're in heaven.
Along came the divers—
now there are...

# 11

eleven.

Spearfishing and scuba diving are popular sports, although today many divers only look at or photograph fish and do not kill them.

Eleven cheeky snappers
racing 'round the bend.
One took a hook—
now there are...

# 10 <sub>ten.</sub>

Recreational fishing, or fishing for fun, has always been a popular pastime. People who fish must be careful not to catch too many, and if they catch undersized fish, they should put them back into the ocean.

Ten dainty clownfish
wondering where to dine.
People started drilling—
now there are . . .

9

nine.

Drilling for oil takes place on, or close to, some reefs throughout the world—fortunately not on Australia's Great Barrier Reef. Oil leaks can also occur, damaging the reef **ecosystems**. Many reefs around the world are mined for building materials, and reefs cannot **regenerate**.

Nine tiny triggerfish
wonderfully ornate.
One found a plastic bag—
now there are ...

# 8

eight.

Each day large amounts of trash are tipped into the ocean. Some modern materials do not **disintegrate**. Turtles and whales sometimes think plastic bags are jellyfish and swallow them. Fish, birds, turtles, and seals are often caught in plastic material and choke to death.

Eight weary wrasses
fed by naughty Kevin.
Shouldn't feed the fish—
now there are . . .

7 seven.

Feeding fish different and unusual food can be dangerous.
It upsets their diet and may even poison them.

Seven pretty parrot fish
performing silly tricks.
One ignored a fishnet—
now there are...

# 6 six.

Overfishing can mean that not enough fish are left to breed in proper numbers. Some fish caught in commercial fishing nets are not even wanted by the fishermen.

Six striking tuskfish
glad to be alive.
Pesticides have killed one—
now there are . . .

# 5

five.

**Pesticides** spread on the land can seep into rivers and the sea.
They do not break down in the water and can build up in the
**food chain**, poisoning sea creatures.

Five Moorish idols
longing to explore.
The water's getting muddy—
now there are...

# 4

four.

Coral needs light to be able to grow. If a lot of **silt** runs off into the ocean around the reef, it makes the water muddy, stopping the light from reaching the coral. This is often caused by clearing large areas of vegetation along the coastline.

Four coral cod
behind a coral tree.
A tanker had an oil spill—
now there are...

3      three.

 Damaged ships can leak oil into the sea. Birds, fish, and other sea life, including plants and coral, can be smothered by the oil and die.

Three fairy basslets
swimming into view.
Crashing anchors break their home—
now there are...

# 2

two.

Boats anchoring in the wrong areas of the reef can cause damage by dragging their anchors and breaking off large chunks of coral.

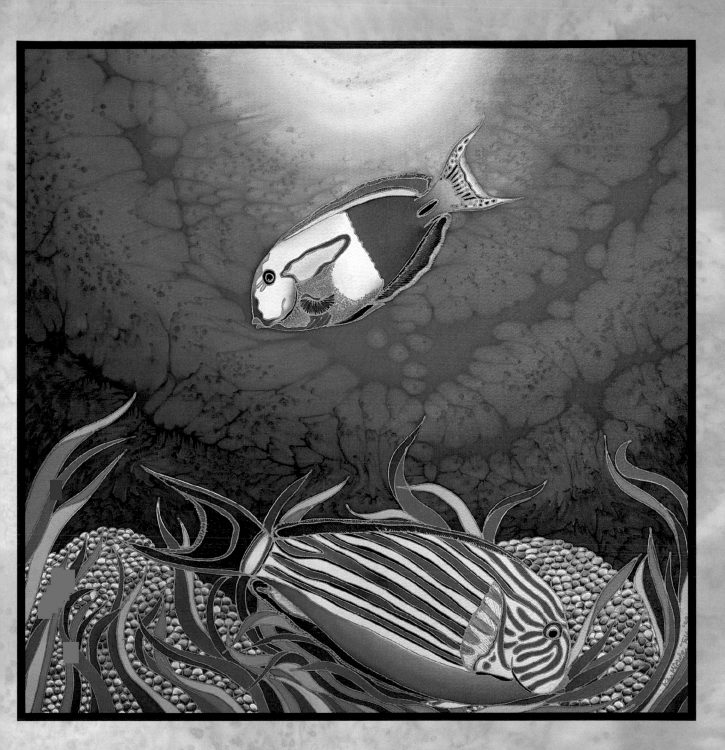

Two hungry surgeonfish
not having any fun.
Little left to eat—
now there is...

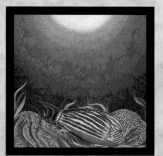

# 1

one.

If the reef **ecosystem** is destroyed, there will be nothing left for sea creatures to live on.

One lonely lionfish
left to be the hero.
No fish left to save—
now there are . . .

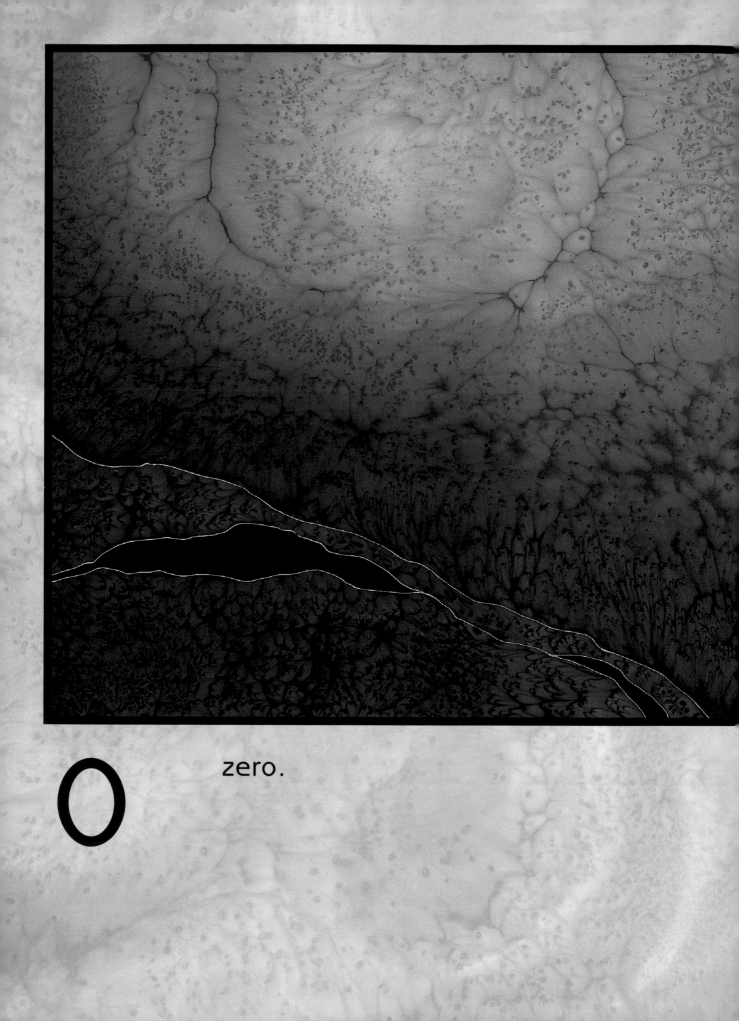

O    zero.

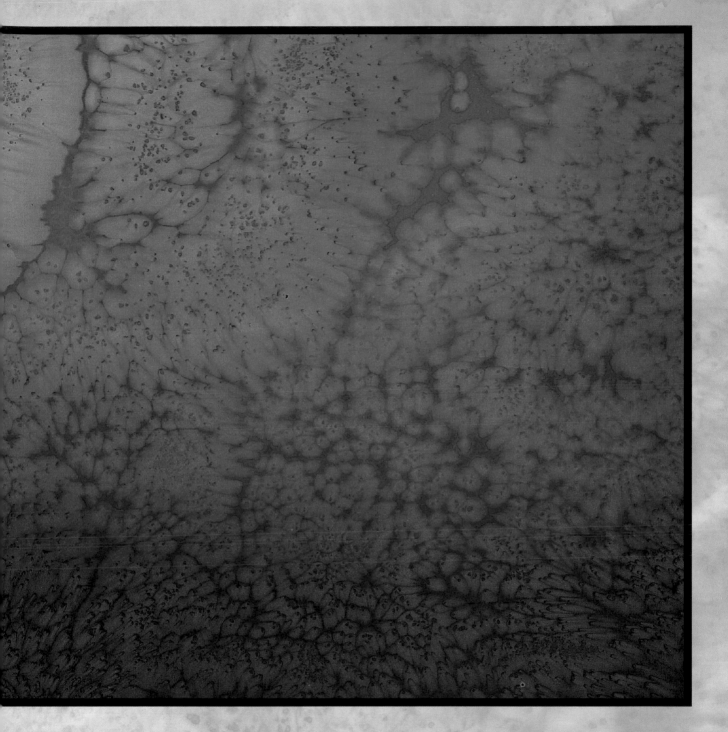

Without constant care we will lose some
of the world's most beautiful natural resources.
Remember: Fish that die one by one
may soon become none.

Thousands of people around Australia and throughout the world have been interested in preserving the beauty and resources of the Great Barrier Reef. They have worked to save the reef itself and to protect the various forms of life—from seaweed to exotic fish—that it supports.

Since 1975 the Great Barrier Reef Marine Park Authority has been successful in protecting this natural treasure. Their guidelines govern the behavior of those who work or play around the reef. By following these guidelines and avoiding the behaviors described in this book, we can all help preserve the Great Barrier Reef and other coral reefs around the world.

# The Fish

## Potato Cod
The potato cod is one of the largest members of the groper family and can weigh up to 650 pounds. The potato cod is extremely curious, which makes it easy for spearfishers to kill it. It eats other fish. It has been declared a **protected species**.

## Angelfish
There are different types of angelfish with different patterns. Also, fish often change their patterns when they become older. Perhaps the prettiest (the one shown in this book) is the imperial angelfish. Angelfish hide among the coral and protect their own area of the reef from other fish. They feed mainly on tube worms.

## Triggerfish
Triggerfish have a long strong first spine that can be locked into place for protection. They have huge heads, which take up one-third of their body size. They eat mainly shellfish.

## Parrot Fish
Parrot fish are members of the wrasse family. Their name comes from the fact that their jaws look like a parrot's beak. They feed on **algae** and bits of coral that they bite off with their strong teeth.

## Tuskfish
The tuskfish is a member of the wrasse family. It has very strong jaws and long bright blue tusklike teeth. It eats smaller fish and shellfish.

## Coral Cod
The coral cod is a member of the groper family. It has a huge mouth and can swallow fish up to half its own size. It hides in the coral, rushing out to catch other fish that it feeds on.

## Surgeonfish
Surgeonfish have one or more sharp spines near the base of their tails, which they use both for attack and defense. They live on **algae**.

## Snappers
Snapper fish have been around for a long time—**fossils** have been found that are 4,700 years old. Snappers swim together in large schools and feed at night on smaller fish.

## Clownfish
Clownfish are the only fish that can live in **sea anemones** without being stung by the anemone's tentacles. The clownfish clean the anemones, which in turn protect them. This is known as a **symbiotic association**. Clownfish feed on **algae** and the leftovers of food in the anemones.

## Wrasses
There is a huge array of shape, size, and color in the wrasse family. They all have thick lips and sharp powerful teeth and feed on other fish by day. Some wrasses are **cleaner fish** for other species.

## Moorish Idols
The Moorish idol is a very striking fish with a protruding snout and small mouth. The snout helps it to forage among cracks in the coral. It eats sea sponges and bits of coral.

## Fairy Basslets
Fairy basslets are tiny, shy, and solitary fish found in deep water. They have an unusual habit of swimming upside down along the roof of an underwater cave. They feed on plant matter.

## Lionfish
Lionfish are members of the cod family. Their spines are extremely poisonous. They are slow swimmers and look like they are floating through the water. They eat smaller fish, which they kill with their poisonous spikes.